STEM Careers

Reinventing ROBOTICS

Saskia Lacey

Consultants

Timothy Rasinski, Ph.D.
Kent State University

Lori Oczkus, M.A.
Literacy Consultant

Publishing Credits

Rachelle Cracchiolo, M.S.Ed., *Publisher*
Conni Medina, M.A.Ed., *Managing Editor*
Dona Herweck Rice, *Series Developer*
Emily R. Smith, M.A.Ed., *Content Director*
Stephanie Bernard/Susan Daddis, M.A.Ed., *Editors*
Robin Erickson, *Senior Graphic Designer*

The TIME logo is a registered trademark of TIME Inc. Used under license.

Image Credits: Cover and p. 1 Chris Willson/Alamy Stock Photo; p. 4 Chris Howes/
Wild Places Photography/Alamy Stock Photo; p. 6 Paul D. Stewart/Science Source; pp.
6–7 PAINTING/Alamy Stock Photo; p. 8 Science Source; pp. 8–9 Ford Motor Company;
p. 11 Chris Willson/Alamy Stock Photo; pp. 12–13 Creative Commons Honda E0-E6 and
P1-P3 by Morio, used under CC BY-SA 3.0; p. 13 catwalker/Shutterstock.com; pp. 14–15
Dakota Fine/The Washington Post via Getty Images; p. 18 Angela Ravaioli/Dreamstime.
com; p. 19 dpa picture alliance archive/Alamy Stock Photo; p. 20 Seoul National
University Biorobotics Laboratory; p. 21 WENN Ltd/Alamy Stock Photo; pp. 22–23 Photo
Courtesy Virginia Tech/Amanda Loman; pp. 24–25 Harvard School of Engineering and
Applied Sciences and Wyss Institute for Biologically Inspired Engineering; pp. 26–27
Daily Mail/Rex/Alamy Stock Photo; p. 28 Andréa Aubert/Science Source; pp. 28–29
Victor Habbick Visions/Science Source; p. 30 ermess/Shutterstock.com; pp. 32–33
Defense Advanced Research Projects Agency; p. 34 urbanbuzz/Alamy Stock Photo; p.
37 Allstar Picture Library/Alamy Stock Photo; pp. 38–39 Peter Cade/Getty Images; pp.
40–41 Adam Taylor/ABC via Getty Images; p. 42 Marilyn Nieves/Getty Images; all other
images from iStock and/or Shutterstock.

All companies and products mentioned in this book are registered
trademarks of their respective owners or developers and are used in this
book strictly for editorial purposes; no commercial claim to their use is
made by the author or the publisher.

Library of Congress Cataloging-in-Publication Data

Names: Lacey, Saskia, author.
Title: STEM careers. Reinventing robotics / Saskia Lacey.
Other titles: Reinventing robotics
Description: Huntington Beach, CA : Teacher Created Materials, Inc., [2017] |
  Audience: Grades 7 to 8. | Includes bibliographical references and index.
Identifiers: LCCN 2016031453 (print) | LCCN 2016034560 (ebook) | ISBN
  9781493836239 (pbk.) | ISBN 9781480757271 (eBook)
Subjects: LCSH: Robots--Juvenile literature. | Robotics--Vocational
  guidance--Juvenile literature.
Classification: LCC TJ211.2 .L33 2017 (print) | LCC TJ211.2 (ebook) | DDC
  629.8/92--dc23
LC record available at https://lccn.loc.gov/2016031453

Teacher Created Materials

5301 Oceanus Drive
Huntington Beach, CA 92649-1030
http://www.tcmpub.com

ISBN 978-1-4938-3623-9

© 2017 Teacher Created Materials, Inc.
Printed in China
WaiMan

Table of Contents

The Robotics Age

Robots are no longer the dream of a distant future. State-of-the-art robots have arrived. There are bots that fly, swim, talk, walk, and even drive. Engineering teams around the world are busy building more sophisticated machines. You can join this team of innovators.

There are thousands of ways to pursue a career in **robotics**. Some **engineers** design bots that are faster and stronger than humans. Others research **androids** that interpret and enhance how humans communicate. Some build robots for mass entertainment—mechanized toys we buy in stores and see on the big screens.

No matter your technology talents, you will find that robotics is a team sport. Designers, engineers, and **programmers**, whether they work in movies or medicine, collaborate to bring their robotic designs to life.

Coining the Term

Science fiction author Isaac Asimov coined the term *robotics* in the 1940s. He was interested in the idea of **artificial** intelligence and featured many robots in his work.

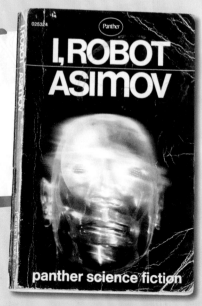

I, ROBOT
ASIMOV

panther science fiction

THINK LINK

- What do you know about the history of robotics and robots from the past?

- How do robots affect daily life today?

- How would the world change if we no longer had computers, which robots rely on to operate?

A Brief History of Bots

Robots are not recent inventions. People have been building machines for centuries. Before we tour the bots of today, let's analyze some of their most primitive **prototypes**.

In the 1500s, Leonardo da Vinci designed a mechanical lion for the king of France. Two hundred years later, Jacques de Vaucanson, a French inventor and artist, built a robotic duck. The mechanical duck appeared to eat and digest grain. These early bots were far ahead of their time. Remember, it wasn't until the twentieth century that the word *robotics* was invented!

Leonardo3 Museum

Leonardo3, a research center in Milan, Italy, currently builds full-scale models of da Vinci's inventions, including his famous flying machines. Some of their exhibitions include little-known designs that are being built for the first time.

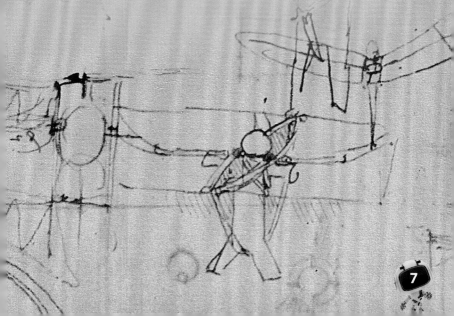

The Original Roboticist

Leonardo da Vinci was a painter, mathematician, and scientist. He was also a **roboticist** and a **visionary**. Da Vinci supported blending fields of study. He viewed science as one of the fine arts.

Da Vinci's notebooks were filled with ideas and inventions that would not be fully realized until centuries after his death. Today, scientists and engineers are still mining his manuscripts for new ideas.

The Rise of Industrial Robots

Henry Ford founded the Ford Motor Company in 1903. He is famous for developing the moving-**chassis** assembly line. Initially, Ford used rope and pulley **conveyor belts** to move an automobile's frame down the assembly line. Later, a mechanized conveyor belt sped up the Model T's rate of production.

Before Ford's invention, it took workers 12 hours to build a single car. By 1914, one Model T could be assembled in about 90 minutes. This moving-chassis assembly line allowed the Ford Motor Company to make cars faster and cheaper than they were before. Eventually, cars became less expensive. More people could enjoy the benefits of travel by car.

Most **industrial** robots have been engineered to speed up production. In 1961, Unimate was designed for General Motors. It was used as a welding machine. The robot also took on the dangerous job of extracting **die-casts**. Robots often do tasks that are thought to be too dirty or unsafe for humans.

Curiosity Rover

NASA's *Curiosity Rover* is searching for signs of life on Mars. The car-size robot is collecting samples of sand and monitoring Martian winds.

Bots of the Space Race

In 1957, the Union of Soviet Socialist Republics (U.S.S.R.) launched the first **orbiting** satellite. The satellite, called *Sputnik*, started a "space race" between the U.S.S.R. and the United States. This competition greatly fueled robotics innovations.

Robots for Support and Sport

Robots have become more than industrial helping machines. Since the late 1980s, decades of research and engineering have focused on developing robots that talk, walk, and think like humans. ASIMO, a humanoid from Honda, is a perfect example of **tenacious** engineering. One of ASIMO's first prototypes was just a pair of robotic legs. Today, the robot can run, hop, and play soccer. The end goal for ASIMO is to one day assist people, such as senior citizens, those who are bedridden, or those in wheelchairs.

Late in the twentieth century, robots became part of pop culture. They were featured in movies and made into toys. Furby, a furry tech toy, was the "it" holiday present of 1998. In Japan, a robot pet named Aibo became a big hit. Engineers at all levels competed in bot battles on the popular television show *Robot Wars*. This show and others like it are still fan favorites. Robots were products that sold well. Engineers raced to build the next robotics breakthroughs.

Robonaut2

The Robonaut2 was the first humanoid to go into space. The bot worked on the International Space Station and completed tasks such as measuring airflow within the spacecraft.

Robosapien

In 2004, Robosapien was created by robotics physicist Dr. Mark W. Tilden. The toy bot was equipped with touch sensors to help it navigate obstacles while walking backward and forward. Later versions included infrared vision. Robosapien could be controlled remotely or operated independently when in "roaming" mode.

Robosapien

The Evolution of ASIMO

Honda engineers began developing the ASIMO humanoid in 1986. The first prototypes weren't pretty, but they taught engineers what they were doing right and what could be improved upon. Examine the time line below.

1986

This version could only walk in a straight line. It sometimes took 20 seconds to take one step!

1987–1991

The next generation of robots walked faster and more naturally. Engineers mimicked how humans shift their weight when they walk.

1991–1993

These robots were engineered to walk up and down sloped surfaces as well as climb stairs.

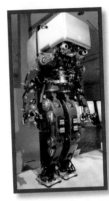

1993–1997

Honda engineers built the robot's arms and upper body. This version becomes the first humanoid robot to walk independently.

2000–Present

The ASIMO robot becomes the most advanced humanoid in the world. The bot can hop, run, and kick. ASIMO will set the standard for humanoid design for years to come.

ASIMO

Modern Robots

Google has developed a super humanoid named Atlas. This search-and-rescue bot is more than six feet (1.8 meters) tall and weighs over 300 pounds (137 kilograms). Mechanical engineers designed, built, and tested Atlas. As a rescue bot, Atlas had to complete a variety of tasks, such as walking on uneven surfaces, picking up boxes, and standing after being pushed to the ground. Because lives could be at risk, Atlas couldn't fail.

In mechanical engineering, every tiny moving part matters. There is always a way to improve a robot's construction. Atlas's mechanical engineers had to think about the robot's mobility and balance. They considered its weight and range of motion. Initially, Atlas was fastened to a computer, which limited where it could go. Even a small change to the robot could have a big impact.

Improving Atlas

The latest version of Atlas has been updated. It is smaller, sleeker, and more agile. Atlas is no longer connected to a computer, which gives it more freedom to move—it now has increased ability to move its wrists. This change, though seemingly minor, opens a world of possibilities. For instance, Atlas can now turn door handles with more ease. This is necessary for a robot that might one day navigate burning buildings!

Finding Your Focus

As an engineer, there are many ways to focus your work in robotics. Do you want to build robots or design them? Do electrical systems interest you? What about software programming? Play to your strengths. Robotics workers are needed in almost every field.

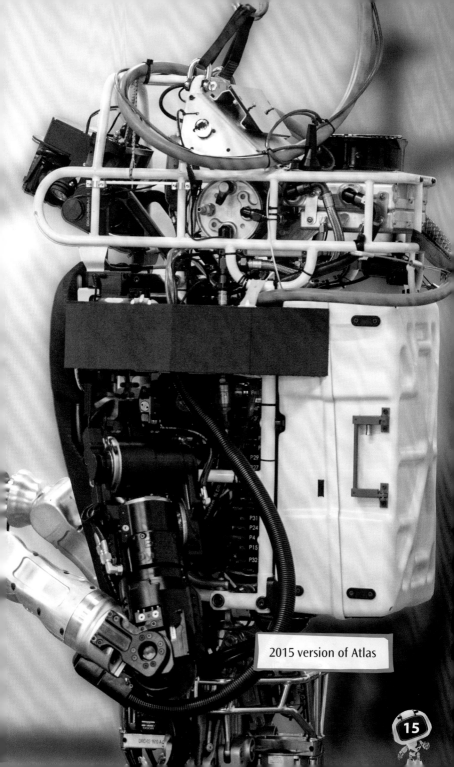

2015 version of Atlas

Robots That Fly

They soar, glide, float, and flutter. These **autonomous** bots range from tiny butterflies to aerial giants. Today's flying machines are some of the most inventive examples of modern robotics.

If you want to work with flying robots, a degree in aerospace engineering will provide you with many options. This field involves the planning, creating, and testing of aircrafts and spacecrafts. Imagine a future where you build rovers, satellites, planes, and drones. The choices are endless!

As an aerospace engineer, you may work with drones. These pilotless aircrafts can be controlled remotely or fly independently. Drones can survey disaster areas and send relief materials to those in need. Businesses are considering using drones as delivery vehicles. There are many benefits of drone technology. But what about their use as weapons? Drones have already become a part of modern warfare. The ability for these flying machines to invade our personal and public spaces can be disturbing.

Delivery—Companies such as Google and Amazon are creating drones to deliver everyday items to people's houses.

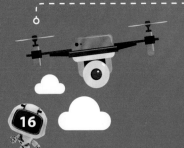

Videography/Photography—Cameras attached to drones make capturing aerial shots easier than before.

Entertainment—Small, toy drones can be bought at stores to play with at home.

Disaster Relief/Aid Efforts—Drones could be used to find missing people in a building collapse, fire, or other situation that may be too dangerous for rescue workers.

STOP! THINK...

- What are some possible positive and negative applications of drone technology?

- What restrictions should there be, if any, on drone usage?

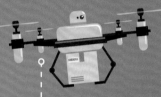

Benefits of Drones

Farming—Drones are used to monitor livestock and crops.

Some of the most impressive flying robots are modeled after living creatures. Festo is a company that designs robots that have been inspired by nature. Some of their products include robotic birds, animals, and insects.

Festo's fluttering robots are known as eMotionButterflies. The butterfly bots have delicate wings made of lightweight, almost sheer, material. Each wing is operated individually. The butterflies use GPS to navigate their surroundings. These mechanical butterflies can even fly in groups, much like real ones. GPS tracks them to help keep them from colliding. The result is a robotic butterfly that looks and acts like the real thing.

SmartBird

FESTO

The SmartBird is another Festo invention. Modeled after the herring gull, this robot flies and moves its wings the way a real bird does. Festo's robotic butterflies and birds are not just beautifully designed but may also have practical applications in the future.

Former German President Christian Wulff holds a SmartBird.

Energy-Saving Bird

Festo's SmartBird weighs a little less than 1 pound (0.45 kilograms) and has a wingspan of 6.5 feet (2 meters). The lightweight design on this bot not only makes flight easier but also helps keep the bot's energy consumption low.

Robots That Swim

Aquatic robots come in all shapes and sizes. Professors Kyu-Jin Cho and Ho-Young Kim, researchers from Seoul National University in South Korea, may have designed one of the smallest robots. Inspired by the water strider insect, their miniature bot can walk on water.

Using high-speed cameras, the two researchers studied the water strider's movements. How was the insect able to "hop" across water? Water striders never break the water's surface tension! When the insect jumps, its legs exert a force on the surface of the water that keep it airborne. The two researchers used this information to build their bot. After much trial and error, they were able to recreate the water strider's unique abilities.

water strider bot

water strider

Mechanical Engineers

These types of engineers design, build, and test robots' structures. They focus on how mechanical parts work together and how outside forces might affect them.

the Crabster, an underwater robot developed in South Korea

Soft-Bodied Aquabots

A robot with fins? Yep! The brilliant brains at the Massachusetts Institute of Technology Computer Science and Artificial Intelligence Laboratory have made a soft-bodied robot that looks and swims like a fish.

Cyro the Robotic Jellyfish

Cyro might be one of the all-time weirdest looking robots. From above, the bot looks like a normal jellyfish. But from below, Cyro is a complex web of wires. The robot was designed at Virginia Tech's College of Engineering.

According to Alex Villanueva, one of Virginia Tech's graduate students, "Cyro has a basic control system. We program Cyro beforehand and basically map out what we want it to do. So when we turn on Cyro in the water, it follows this mission that we pre-programmed." The mechanical engineering team behind Cyro hopes that one day the robot will be used for a variety of missions. Cyro is funded by the U.S. Navy. Maybe it will be used as a deep-sea spy!

The Benthic Rover

While *Curiosity Rover* explores Martian landscapes, deep-sea rovers investigate the mysteries of our ocean floor. In 2009, the Benthic Rover spent months underwater tracking how deep-sea organisms are affected by environmental changes at the surface.

Working with Aquabots

There are engineers who work primarily with marine robots. They use autonomous underwater vehicles to study the ocean's environment.

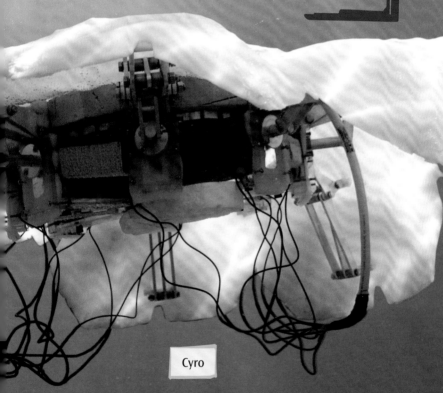

Cyro

By Air or Sea!

Harvard University's mechanical bee is the same size as its living inspiration. But, unlike a real bee, the robot can use its wings to propel through air *and* water.

Designing the RoboBee presented a number of challenges. Because the mechanical bee is small and light, it had difficulty breaking through the water's surface tension. A substance that reduces surface tension, known as a surfactant, was added to the bee's wings. Even with this substance, the RoboBee can only enter the water by diving into the surface at top speed.

RoboBee

Swumanoid the Humanoid

The Swumanoid, an aquatic humanoid, is able to swim the backstroke, the front crawl, and the butterfly. Scientists envision machines similar to Swumanoid being used as robot lifeguards.

RoboBee Inventors

In August 2012, Kevin Y. Ma and Robert J. Wood designed the RoboBee. They worked on this project at the Harvard School of Engineering and Applied Sciences and Wyss Institute for Biologically Inspired Engineering.

The RoboBee uses the same basic **mechanics** to navigate underwater as it does in the air. One of the only differences is its wing speed. In the air, the mechanical bee flaps its wings 120 times per second; in the water, it only flaps 9 times per second. Engineers and researchers at Harvard are still trying to improve the bee's transition between air and water.

Robots That Heal

Robots have changed modern healthcare. There are bionic limbs and surgical robots. The realities of science are beginning to look a lot like science fiction.

A bionic **prosthetic** is a type of medical robot. The word *bionic* means having artificial body parts. There are several parts to every bionic prosthetic. These parts are the biosensors, mechanical sensors, controllers, and **actuators**.

Biosensors monitor nervous and muscle systems. They "sense" the wearer's intentions. They predict what the wearer wants to do, such as taking a step forward.

Mechanical sensors monitor the medical device itself. Both types of sensors send information to the controller. Then, the controller sends this information to an actuator. The actuator is an artificial muscle. It may aid or completely replace the wearer's original muscle tissue.

Robotic Pills

The Rani capsule may one day replace injectable medicines such as insulin. Inside the capsule are needles of sugar that push through a patient's intestinal walls, delivering medicine directly to the bloodstream.

Bionic Exoskeletons

A bionic exoskeleton is an example of a bionic prosthetic. It is a wearable bionic suit that enables paralyzed people to walk. The exoskeleton's sensors activate when a user shifts his or her weight. Battery-powered actuators drive each foot forward.

Robot Surgeons

Imagine a robot so precise that it can peel grapes and fold origami. The da Vinci® Surgical System is one such machine. This medical robot performs a variety of operations with instruments that gives surgeons more control. These instruments can bend in ways that human hands cannot. This makes the surgical process more efficient.

The da Vinci robot can perform different types of cardiac surgery. With the help of the robot, doctors can complete heart surgeries with just a few small incisions. Without the robot, the surgeons would need to make large incisions to reach small or tight areas of the body. This would likely result in longer recovery times for patients.

The da Vinci robot is also helping pave the way for remote surgery. This means that a doctor in New York would be able to conduct a surgery on a patient in California.

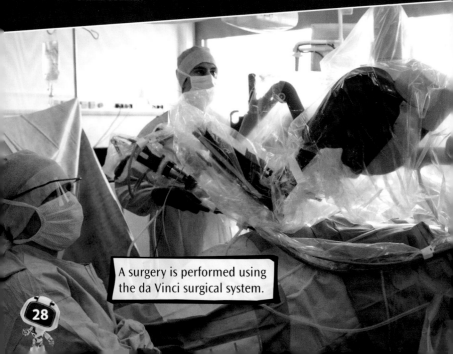

A surgery is performed using the da Vinci surgical system.

Microrobots

Smaller than a millimeter, star-shaped robots called *microrobots* are able to perform biopsies. A biopsy is when a sample of tissue is removed and studied. Known as *microgrippers*, the robot's "arms" close around tissue when activated by body heat.

artist's version of microrobot

THINK LINK

◎ What might robotic healthcare look like?

◎ Do you think the existence of robot nurses and doctors is a positive or negative possibility? Why?

◎ What do you predict will be a development in the field of medical robotics?

Robots That Drive

Remote-controlled cars and trucks have been around for years. But today, engineers are developing a new prototype that may not need a remote. What if cars could drive themselves? How would that change our world? Thanks to the work of researchers and engineers across the country, we are learning the answers to these questions.

The first driverless car competition, the DARPA Grand Challenge, took place in 2004. (DARPA stands for Defense Advanced Research Projects Agency.) The competition was largely a failure. No team crossed the finish line to claim the cash prize. But the competition set in motion the race to create an autonomous vehicle.

Come 2005, the teams were more prepared. They had analyzed what went wrong with their vehicles in the previous race and made adjustments. Their redesigned vehicles were ready to take on the 130 miles (209.2 kilometers) of desert terrain.

Hardware vs. Software

Every robot has hardware and software. A robot's hardware is its physical structure, the parts and pieces you can see and touch. Software is the robot's electrical systems or computer programming. It helps the machine interpret its environment. A robot can *look* great, but it needs software to *do* something great.

Robotics Controls Engineer

A controls engineer is in charge of how robots are "controlled." They design the software that brings bots to life. Controls engineers usually have degrees in electrical engineering or mechanical engineering.

There were two front-runners in DARPA's 2005 Grand Challenge. Carnegie Mellon University's H1ghlander and Stanford University's Stanley. The teams behind each of the robots had different approaches to the race. H1ghlander's engineers focused on the hardware of their vehicle.

The New Commuter

Google's autonomous car is ready to hit the road—legally. In 2016, the National Highway Safety Traffic Association said the car's self-driving system is a legal driver. Soon, people may have the chance to let these cars navigate traffic for them.

Stanley's engineers focused on their robot's software. Their vehicle had a vision system that was able to read the surrounding terrain. Stanley could perceive immediate and long-range obstacles. This allowed the vehicle to avoid collisions and maintain its course.

In the end, Stanley's software proved to be a great asset, and it placed first. But the Grand Challenge was a success for many teams. Five vehicles crossed the finish line. During the previous year's DARPA challenge, not one vehicle finished the race!

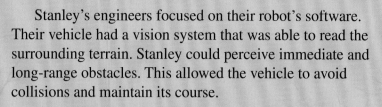

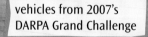

vehicles from 2007's DARPA Grand Challenge

Elon Musk

Tesla. SpaceX. Paypal. Sound familiar? Each company is the billion-dollar brainchild of inventor and entrepreneur Elon Musk. The aforementioned companies are just the beginning. Musk plans to colonize Mars within the next 20 years.

Robots That Entertain

On the big screen, robots are often presented as destructive androids that crave world domination. Artificial intelligence has long been seen as the ultimate threat to humanity. From Robocop to Ultron, our perspective of talking technology has been largely negative. But there are a few cinematic exceptions. The Star Wars Series, for example, has created lovable robots for decades.

In a Galaxy Far, Far Away. . .

R2-D2, the astromech droid, might be one of the most beloved bots of all time. Audiences of all ages delight in the robot's expressive bleeps and bloops. Ralph McQuarrie, the concept artist behind the "look" of Star Wars, designed R2-D2, while engineer Tony Dyson was responsible for building the original droid. According to Dyson, he built eight R2-D2s! Some of the bots were remote controlled; others were computerized. BB-8, the bot from *Star Wars: The Force Awakens*, is based on the earlier work of McQuarrie and Dyson.

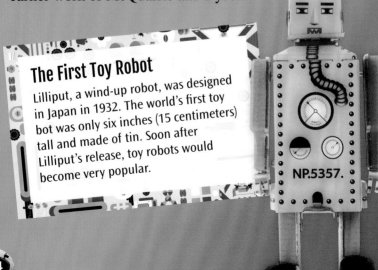

The First Toy Robot

Lilliput, a wind-up robot, was designed in Japan in 1932. The world's first toy bot was only six inches (15 centimeters) tall and made of tin. Soon after Lilliput's release, toy robots would become very popular.

NP.5357.

The Perfect Pet

Aibo, Sony's robotic dog, was envisioned as the ideal pet. The bot could learn your likes and dislikes and would entertain and comfort you depending on your moods. The final version of Aibo could play fetch and follow voice commands.

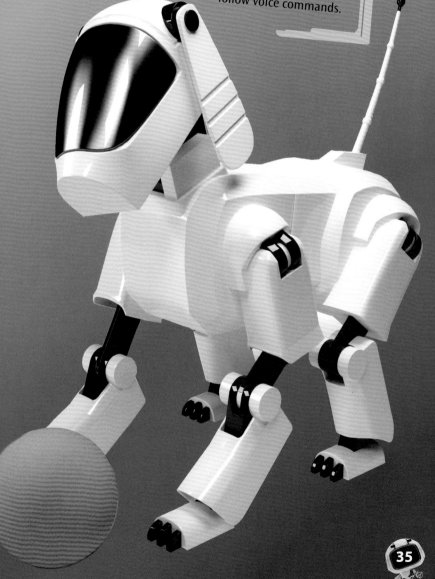

Minds Behind the Machine

Roboticists are often presented with problems. They work together, combining their areas of expertise to find solutions. Sometimes, solving problems creates more problems; sometimes, it creates solutions to different problems. This is the story of BB-8's journey from concept to construction.

J. J. Abrams (director of *Star Wars: The Force Awakens*)

Abrams drew the initial BB-8 sketch on a napkin. "I named him BB-8 because it was almost onomatopoeia," Abrams said. "It was sort of how he looked to me, with the 8, obviously, and then the 2 B's."

Christian Alzmann (concept designer)

Alzmann worked as a concept designer for the robot. Alzmann said, "J. J. wanted something rolling on a sphere, so I tried a lot of different designs developing that idea. Ultimately, BB-8 developed out of a back-and-forth process with J. J., where he gave feedback on each iteration of the design."

Jake Lunt Davies (concept designer)

Davies built upon Alzmann's vision for BB-8. He tried many different structures before settling on a half-dome head and spherical body.

Neal Scanlan (animatronics and special effects artist)

Scanlan and his team made the aliens and robots featured in *The Force Awakens*. But building BB-8 presented unique problems. Scanlan said, "In the case of BB-8, we couldn't make any concessions, as the design already existed as a hemisphere on a ball. So, our challenge was bringing this to the screen."

Joshua Lee (senior animatronic designer)

Lee, a member of Scanlan's team, was responsible for building BB-8's body. "I made a little puppet version," said Lee. "I remember as soon as I picked that up, it was just so expressive."

Dave Chapman and Brian Herring (puppeteers)

Chapman and Herring helped create BB-8's personality. According to Herring, "BB-8 can cock his head over and look away, he can double take, he can look scared, he can look angry. We managed to find a whole vocabulary of movement for him."

Matthew Denton (electronic design and development supervisor)

Denton developed the electronic design of BB-8. He and Lee worked together to create a series of specialized BB-8 props. Some bots were made for close-ups. Some were remote controlled. Others were puppeteered by Chapman and Herring.

After the Credits

The BB-8 models used in *The Force Awakens* were impressive but not fully functional. Lee wanted to build a BB-8 that moved independently, without puppetry. After much research and multiple prototypes, Lee debuted the robot at a panel for the movie. The audience went wild. Many people thought that BB-8 was a product of computer-generated imagery. Lee had proved them wrong!

Junior Engineers

Vast, complex, and ever changing, the field of robotics is similar to the human imagination. As our tech-dependent world becomes increasingly automated, jobs in robotics will become more and more specialized. The need for new ideas and innovations is growing.

It's never too early to get started on your career in robotics. Many students assume that the time to think about the future is when they are in college. Not so. If you have an interest in robotics, explore the possibilities. Do you want to work on rovers and satellites? Or are humanoids more your speed? The earlier you define your dream, the more likely you will be able to make a plan to achieve it!

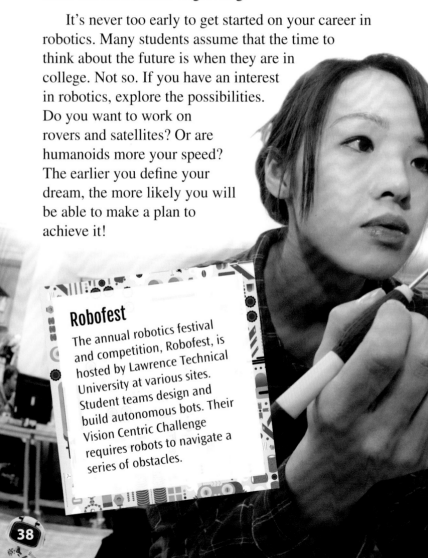

Robofest

The annual robotics festival and competition, Robofest, is hosted by Lawrence Technical University at various sites. Student teams design and build autonomous bots. Their Vision Centric Challenge requires robots to navigate a series of obstacles.

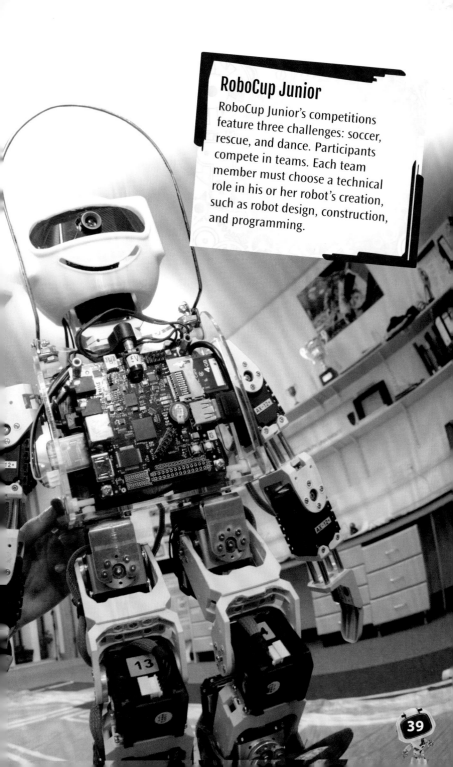

RoboCup Junior

RoboCup Junior's competitions feature three challenges: soccer, rescue, and dance. Participants compete in teams. Each team member must choose a technical role in his or her robot's creation, such as robot design, construction, and programming.

Getting Your Foot in the Door

Budding roboticists often get their start in robotics clubs at school. Sometimes, student groups enter the robots they build into competitions. Being part of a robotics club and designing your own bots gives you an advantage over less-experienced students when it comes time to apply for colleges and **internships**.

For any competitive field, interning is a *really* good idea. It will help you get to know people in your industry and likely pave the way for future jobs. Internships are usually unpaid. Pick your dream company, and research how you might work for them. High school isn't far away, so plan your summer internships in advance. Don't be afraid to think outside the box.

Choosing Your Dream Internship

Get an inside look at robotics giants, such as Apple Inc. or NASA, as an intern. Apple has a month-long engineering camp for high school students in Cupertino, California. NASA internship opportunities run throughout the year.

FIRST Robotics Competition

Participants in the FIRST Lego® League build robots using Lego Mindstorms kits. Each year, teams focus on global problems and must collaborate to produce solutions. In 2015, the problem was what to do with trash and recycling. Students had to design recycling bots that transferred and sorted Lego blocks.

The Future's Future

Our world is evolving at a rapid pace, and engineering is leading the charge. The time gap between the introduction of different game-changing technologies has closed to such a degree that the "next big thing" seems to come along on the heels of the previous one. This reality is never more apparent than in the field of robotics. Because there are robotics applications for all of society's demands—from health to defense to entertainment—the need for better, faster, and more adept robotics is a constant.

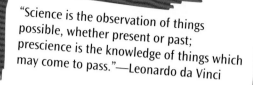

Robots in the Classroom?

How would you enjoy learning about geometry using a robot? A company called RobotsLab has created a box full of little bots that help teach math, science, and technology. Maybe one day, classrooms all over will have robots!

If there were ever a time for skilled engineers to show what they can do, that time is now. The field is wide open, and well-trained roboticists will likely have their pick of job opportunities.

Creating the Cutting Edge

But here's the trick. If the future is happening now, and the machines we've imagined for decades are in production, what's ahead? How do we invent what we haven't dreamed of yet? The future of robotics demands fresh perspectives. Like the visionaries of the past, the next generation of engineers must design the new impossible. Da Vinci did it, so why can't you?

Glossary

actuators—mechanical devices used to help move or control something

androids—robots in the forms of human beings

artificial—made by human skill; not natural

autonomous—having the ability to act independently

chassis—the steel framework of an automobile

conveyor belts—bands or chains for carrying materials or objects short distances

die-casts—shapes created by pouring molten metal into molds

engineers—people trained and skilled in the design, construction, and use of engines or machines

humanoid—having human characteristics; resembling human beings

industrial—related to or resulting from industry

internships—any official or formal programs to provide practical experience for beginners in an occupation or profession

mechanics—the technical aspect or working parts; structure

orbiting—traveling along the curved path, usually elliptical, of a planet, satellite, spaceship, etc., around a celestial body, such as the sun

programmers—people who write computer programs

prosthetic—a device that substitutes for a missing or damaged limb

prototypes—originals or models on which something is based or formed

roboticist—a specialist in robots or robotics

robotics—the branch of technology that deals with the design, construction, operation, and application of robots

tenacious—persistent, not easily discouraged

visionary—a person of unusually keen foresight

Index

Check It Out!

Books

Asimov, Isaac. 2008. *I, Robot*. Spectra.

Ishogawa, Yoshito. 2014. *The Lego Mindstorms EV3 Idea Book: 181 Simple Machines and Clever Contraptions*. No Starch Press.

Meyer, Marissa. 2013. *Cinder*. Square Fish.

Platt, Charles. 2015. *Make: Electronics: Learning Through Discovery, 2nd Edition*. Maker Media, Inc.

Wilson, Daniel H. 2015. *Popular Mechanics Robots: A New Age of Bionics*. Hearst Books.

Videos

The Great Robot Race. PBS. http://www.pbs.org/wgbh /nova/darpa/.

Websites

American Honda Motor Co. Inc. *INSIDE ASIMO*. http://asimo.honda.com/inside-asimo/.

DARPA. *Defense Advanced Research Projects Agency*. http://www.darpa.mil.

For Inspiration & Recognition of Science & Technology. *First Robotics Competition*. http://www.firstinspires .org/robotics/frc.

Try It!

You've been hired by your school district to design a robot to support students, faculty, and staff in some way.

◎ What problem will your robot help solve? How will it help people on a day-to-day basis?

◎ Design your robot by hand or on the computer. Will it be humanoid?

◎ Give your robot a name similar to the robots referred to in this reader.

◎ What rules will you program into this robot to ensure it won't harm anyone?

About the Author

Saskia Lacey is the author of *Jurassic Classics: The Prehistoric Masters of Literature* and *Technical Tales: How to Build a Plane* as well as several other books. She has written about prehistoric presidents, mice mechanics, and reptilian writers. Someday, she hopes to write a book about the history of the humanoid.